QUICK & EASY
Sewing

QUICK & EASY
Sewing

Stylish, speedy designs
for your home

Emma Hardy

CICO BOOKS
LONDON NEW YORK

Dedication

This book is dedicated to my Mum,
who taught me to sew.

NOTE:
Unless otherwise stated, all fabric quantities
given in the projects are based on fabric that
is 54 in (135 cm) wide.

This edition published in 2024 by CICO Books
An imprint of Ryland Peters & Small Ltd
20–21 Jockey's Fields   341 E 116th St
London WC1R 4BW   New York, NY 10029
www.rylandpeters.com

10 9 8 7 6 5 4 3 2 1

First published in 2008 as *Sewing in No Time*

Text © Emma Hardy 2024
Design, photography, and illustration ©
CICO Books 2024

A CIP catalog record for this book is available from the
Library of Congress and the British Library.

ISBN: 978-1-80065-335-1

Printed in China

Editor: Sarah Hoggett
Designer: David Fordham
Illustrator: Michael Hill
Photographer: Debbie Patterson
Stylist: Emma Hardy

Editorial assistant: Danielle Rawlings
Art director: Sally Powell
Senior designer: Emily Breen
Creative director: Leslie Harrington
Production manager: Gordana Simakovic
Publishing manager: Carmel Edmonds

Contents

Introduction

I've enjoyed sewing ever since I was a child. My mother taught me the basic stitches, which I used to make doll's clothes, blankets, and costumes by hand, progressing to making my own clothes as I got older and had mastered the sewing machine. I loved being able to create designs that were unique, individual, and allowed me to express myself.

I still very much delight in this process—but these days, the demands of modern life mean that I am short of time. With this in mind, I have put together 35 projects that are quick and easy to make. From bed linen and pillows to window treatments, storage ideas, and table linen, the projects are both practical and decorative and most can be made in a matter of hours. A basic sewing kit and sewing machine are all that you need, and most of the projects are ideal for a novice—although I hope that the designs will appeal to the experienced stitcher as well as the beginner.

Each beautifully photographed design is accompanied by charmingly illustrated instructions that lead you step by step through the projects. Each project also includes an estimated timing, although this is only a guide: the actual time will vary depending on your experience and expertise. The techniques section at the back of the book gives a simple guide to basic skills and the book also contains all the templates that you need to complete the projects.

Choose fabrics that will complement and coordinate with your décor and home furnishings, or tailor-make projects to create special gifts for friends and family. Experiment with colors, patterns, and trimmings, collecting ribbons, braids, and vintage buttons to give your creations the perfect finishing touches. With such a wide selection of wonderful fabrics currently on sale from craft and sewing shops and online companies, I hope you will be inspired to use this book as a starting point to create your own designs.

CHAPTER 1

Relaxation spaces

Floral throw pillow with ties

each cover 1½ hours

Add a pretty, country feel to your couch with these lovely floral pillows. I used the same fabric throughout, but you could choose a coordinating fabric for the back, so that you can turn the pillow over and change the look to suit your mood.

The covers are very easy to make, as they have no zippers or buttons but are fastened with neat little fabric ties. To make them even simpler, you could replace the ties with ribbon.

YOU WILL NEED

30 in (75 cm) floral fabric

Sewing machine and matching sewing thread

18 in (45 cm) square pillow form (pad)

Take ½ in (1.5 cm) seam allowances throughout unless otherwise stated.

1. Cut a piece of fabric measuring 19 x 19¼ in (48 x 49 cm). Along one short edge, fold over ⅜ in (1 cm) and then another ½ in (1.5 cm) to the wrong side. Machine stitch in place.

2. Cut four 3 x 10 in (7 x 25 cm) strips of fabric. Fold each one in half, wrong sides together, and press. Open out. Along both long sides, fold over ½ in (1.5 cm) to the wrong side and press. At one short end, fold over ½ in (1.5 cm) and press.

3. Fold the whole strip in half along the center fold line. Machine stitch along the strip, stitching as close to the unfolded edge as possible, and across the folded end. Press.

4. Cut a 19 x 7½ in (48 x 19 cm) rectangle of fabric. Along one long edge, fold over ⅜ in (1 cm) and then another ½ in (1.5 cm) to the wrong side. Pin and machine stitch.

5. Cut a 19 in (48 cm) square of fabric. With right sides together, pin the raw edge of the rectangle from Step 4 to one side of the square, inserting one tie into the seam 4½ in (12 cm) from one corner and another one 4½ in (12 cm) from the other corner. Machine stitch in place. Press the seam open.

6. Lay this piece wrong side down on your work surface. With right sides together, place the other piece of fabric from Step 1 on top, aligning the hemmed side with the seam on the bottom piece.

7. Fold the flap over the top and pin and machine stitch around the three sides of the square. Turn the cover right side out.

8. Take the remaining two ties, fold under ½ in (1.5 cm) at the raw ends and machine stitch them onto the pillow cover, aligning them with the ties already in place. Press the cover. insert the pillow form (pad) and tie the ties in a neat bow to close.

Dotty patchwork pillow

2 hours

Stitch large circles of patterned fabric onto plain linen to make this delightfully dotty pillow cover. Choose scraps of your favorite fabrics for the dots and edge them with a small zigzag stitch to prevent them from fraying.

YOU WILL NEED

Compass, pencil, and paper for pattern

10 in (25 cm) each of a selection of patterned fabrics

20 in (50 cm) natural-colored linen

18 in (45 cm) square pillow form (pad)

14 in (35 cm) zipper

Sewing machine and matching sewing thread

1. Using a compass, draw a circle 5 in (13 cm) in diameter on paper. Cut out and use as a paper pattern. Pin to the fabrics and cut out nine fabric circles.

2. Cut two 19 in (48 cm) squares of linen. Lay one piece right side up on your work surface and arrange the fabric circles on top, leaving $3/8$ in (1 cm) between each one and $1\frac{1}{2}$ in (3.5 cm) all the way around the edge. Using a small zigzag stitch on the sewing machine, stitch all around the fabric circles staying as close to the edge as you can.

3. With right sides together, baste (tack) the two linen squares together along one side using the seam allowance. Machine stitch from each corner for 2 in (5 cm). Press the seam open and lay the zipper right side down on the wrong side of the seam. Baste and then machine stitch the zipper in place. Remove the basting stitches.

4. With right sides together, pin and machine stitch the remaining three sides of the fabric squares together. Snip the corners, open the zipper, and turn the pillow cover right side out. Press. Insert the pillow form (pad).

Throw pillow with ribbon stripes

This is the perfect way to use up all those leftover bits of ribbon that never seem to be quite long enough to be useful. Collect together ribbons and braids in similar colors and stitch them onto plain fabric to make a stylish pillow cover that no one would guess was made from scraps.

YOU WILL NEED

20 in (50 cm) plain fabric

Selection of ribbons in toning colors and various widths

Sewing machine

Matching sewing thread

13¾ x 20 in (35 x 50 cm) pillow form (pad)

3 buttons

Take ½ in (1.5 cm) seam allowances throughout unless otherwise stated.

1. Cut two 15¾ x 15¼ in (40 x 39 cm) rectangles of plain fabric. Fold over and press ⅜ in (1 cm) to the wrong side along one 15¾ in (40 cm) edge of each piece. Fold over another ½ in (1.5 cm) on one piece and 2 in (5 cm) on the other and machine stitch close to the edge.

2. Make three buttonholes along this wider border (see page 120) to fit the size of the buttons you are using.

3. Cut a 15 x 21 in (38 x 53 cm) rectangle of plain fabric. Lay it on your work surface and place the ribbons on it until you are happy with the arrangement. Pin them in place, then baste (tack) and machine stitch each one onto the fabric.

4. Lay the ribbon-covered piece right side up on your work surface, with the buttonholed back piece right side down on top, aligning the raw edges. Place the other back piece right side down on top, again aligning the raw edges, and pin in place. Machine stitch around the edges, trim the corners to reduce bulk, and turn right side out. Sew three buttons onto the back in the required position. Press. Insert the pillow form (pad).

YOU WILL NEED

10 in (25 cm) lengths of a selection of small-patterned fabrics

Paper for template

Pencil and compass

Needle and thread

Store-bought pillow cover to fit 14 in (35 cm) square pad

14 in (35 cm) square pillow form (pad)

Yo-yo throw pillow

This is the perfect introduction to simple sewing. The yo-yos are made from scraps of patterned fabric, stitched onto a store-bought cover to create an inexpensive but very decorative pillow. If you're making a pillow in a different size, remember that the finished yo-yos will be about half the size of the original circle. It's also best to make all the yo-yos from the same weight of fabric; lightweight dress cotton is ideal.

Rosettes: 5 minutes each; Whole project: 4 hours

1. Using a compass, draw a circle 4¾ in (12 cm) in diameter on paper. Cut out and pin the template onto your fabric. Cut out 36 circles from a variety of fabrics. Turn over about ¼ in (5 mm) to the wrong side and press all the way around.

2. Work a line of running stitches around each circle close to the fold. Pull the thread to gather and secure with a few stitches.

3. Arrange the rosettes on your work surface in six rows of six, making sure that no two rosettes of the same fabric are next to one another. Stitch each row together with a few small stitches, and then stitch the six rows together in the same way to form a panel.

4. Lay the panel on the front of the pillow cover and hand stitch it in place by working a few stitches at the widest point of each rosette and a few stitches around the inner edges to hold everything securely in place.

Floral floor rug

For a quick-and-easy way to bring pattern into a room without completely redecorating, why not make this pretty fireside rug? Made from vintage-style, floral fabric edged with a ruffled border that picks up one of the colors in the main fabric, it is as decorative as it is useful. A wide velvet ribbon in a contrast color provides a lovely finishing touch. Choose a heavyweight furnishing fabric that will withstand a bit of wear and tear.

YOU WILL NEED

20 in (50 cm) plain fabric for the frill

40 in (1 m) heavyweight floral cotton or furnishing fabric

60 in (1.5 m) velvet ribbon

Sewing machine

Needle and matching sewing thread

Take ½ in (1.5 cm) seam allowances throughout unless otherwise stated.

1. Cut two 6 x 59 in (15 x 150 cm) strips of plain fabric for the frill. With right sides together, fold in half lengthwise and machine stitch along both short ends. Turn right side out and press. Work a line of running stitches about ⅜ in (1 cm) from the raw edge along the whole length. Pull the thread to gather the fabric so that the frill is 21¼ in (54 cm) long. Secure with a few stitches at the end.

2. Cut two 22½ x 29½ in (57 x 75 cm) rectangles of floral fabric and two 23½ in (60 cm) lengths of velvet ribbon. Pin and machine stitch one ribbon onto each short end of one of the floral pieces 2 in (5 cm) from the edge.

3. With right sides together, aligning the raw edges, lay one frill along each short end of the floral fabric to which you stitched the ribbon. Pin and baste (tack) in place.

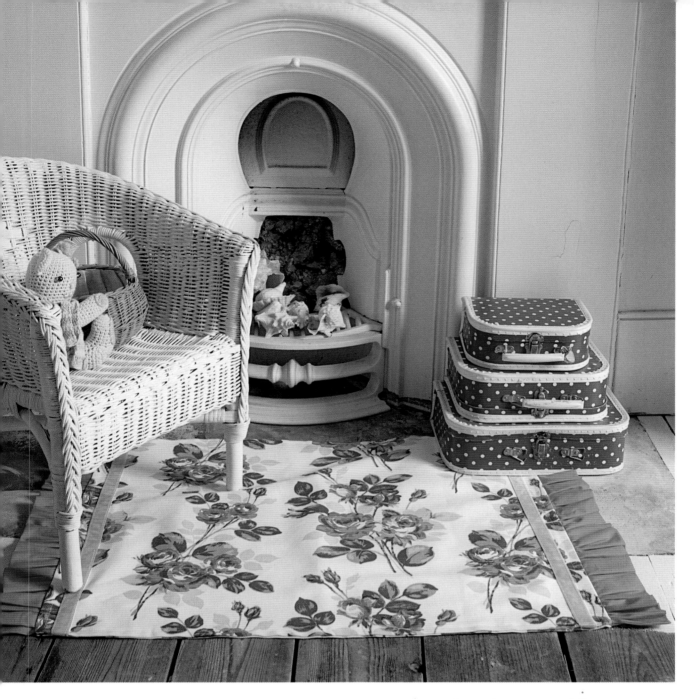

4. With right sides together, lay the other floral piece on top. Pin and machine stitch all the way around, leaving an 8 in (20 cm) opening along one long side. Trim the corners, turn right side out, and press. Hand stitch the opening closed. Topstitch all the way around the rug ³⁄₈ in (1 cm) from the edge.

Simple drape with patterned border

Liven up a plain drape (curtain) with patterned borders and braids or use this method to lengthen existing drapes to fit a new window. Choose fabrics with similar colors, mixing spots, stripes, and florals, and add ricrac braid and ribbon for extra decoration.

3 hours

YOU WILL NEED

Spotted fabric

20 in (50 cm) striped fabric

20 in (50 cm) floral fabric

Sewing machine and matching thread

Two lengths of braid

One length of jumbo ricrac braid

Drape (curtain) lining fabric

Drape (curtain) heading tape

Take ½ in (1.5 cm) seam allowances throughout unless otherwise stated.

1. Cut a piece of spotted fabric to the required size. Cut a piece of striped fabric 10¼ in (26 cm) deep and a piece of floral fabric 11½ in (29 cm) deep; both pieces should be the same width as the spotted fabric. With right sides together, pin and machine stitch the striped fabric to the bottom of the spotted fabric and the floral fabric to the bottom of the striped fabric. Press open the seams.

2. Pin and machine stitch one piece of braid over the join between the floral and striped fabrics. Pin and stitch the ricrac braid along the join between the striped and spotted fabrics. Lay the second piece of braid over half of the ricrac and stitch in place.

3. Cut a piece of lining fabric the same length as the drape (curtain) and 1¼ in (3 cm) narrower. With right sides together, pin and machine stitch the lining fabric to the drape along both long sides. Turn right side out and press.

4. At the top of the drape (curtain), turn over ⅜ in (1 cm) to the wrong side. Turn over an additional 2 in (5 cm) and pin. Pin the drape heading tape along this folded section and machine stitch in place. Hem the bottom of the drape by folding over ⅜ in (1 cm) and another 1¼ in (3 cm) and machine stitch in place.

CHAPTER 2

Kitchens and dining rooms

Cutlery roll

2 hours

This is the perfect way to store a set of cutlery, to prevent the individual pieces from getting scratched and keep all the components together. Alternatively, use it to keep picnic cutlery handy for *al fresco* dining so that you're always ready for an impromptu summer outing. Careful measuring is essential, to ensure that the compartments are evenly spaced across the roll.

YOU WILL NEED

20 in (50 cm) patterned fabric

20 in (50 cm) polka-dot fabric

34 in (86 cm) length of 1 in (22 mm) wide grosgrain ribbon

Sewing machine

Needle and matching sewing thread

Take ½ in (1.5 cm) seam allowances throughout unless otherwise stated.

1. Cut a 24½ x 4¾ in (62 x 12 cm) rectangle of polka-dot fabric and a 24½ x 2¼ in (62 x 6 cm) strip of patterned fabric. With right sides together, aligning raw edges, lay the patterned fabric along one long edge of the polka-dot strip and machine stitch ½ in (1.5 cm) in from the edge. Fold the patterned strip over, turn under, and press ½ in (1.5 cm) along the remaining raw edge, and slipstitch in place along the back.

2. Cut a 24½ x 13 in (62 x 33 cm) rectangle of polka-dot fabric. Lay the patterned border piece along one long edge, with the raw edges together at the bottom. Measure 2¼ in (6 cm) in from one side and pin from the top to the bottom of the smaller panel. Continue along the panel, pinning every 2 in (5 cm). There will be another 2¼ in (6 cm) pocket at the other end. Machine stitch along each pinned line.

3. Cut a 34 in (86 cm) length of blue grosgrain ribbon. Cut a 26¼ x 15¼ in (67 x 39 cm) piece of patterned fabric. Pin the ribbon across the fabric 5 in (13 cm) from the bottom and 1½ in (3.5 cm) from the edge, leaving the same amount of ribbon extending beyond each edge. Machine stitch the ribbon onto the fabric, stitching a rectangle 4¾ in (12 cm) long to fix the ribbon securely in place.

4. With wrong sides together, center the polka-dot panel on the patterned fabric, leaving an even border all the way around. Fold the corners over and fold each side of the patterned fabric over by ³⁄₈ in (1 cm) and then by another ½ in (1.5 cm). Pin, baste (tack), and machine stitch in place, stitching as close to the folded edge as possible.

1. Cut a 7 x 10 in (18 x 25 cm) piece of patterned fabric and two 2½ x 10 in (6.5 x 25 cm) pieces of plain fabric. With right sides together, lay each plain piece along one long side of the patterned piece. Pin and machine stitch together. Press the seams open.

Pan holder

This practical pan holder is very straightforward to make and requires only limited sewing skills. Choose a bold pattern for a striking look and line with thick batting (wadding) to provide adequate protection from the heat. Hang it up by the fabric loop and it will always be on hand when you need it.

2. Cut two 10¼ in (26 cm) squares of thick batting (wadding). Place the backing fabric wrong side up on your work surface, with the batting squares on top and the front of the cover right side up on top of the batting. Pin all layers together. Stick a piece of masking tape diagonally from one corner to the other and machine stitch along the edge of the tape. Reposition the tape 1¼ in (3 cm) from the stitching line. Stitch along the edge. Continue until you reach the corner. Lay masking tape across the other two corners and repeat the stitching process until the whole mat is quilted.

| 1½ hours |

YOU WILL NEED

40 in (1 m) patterned fabric

10 in (25 cm) plain fabric

20 in (50 cm) thick batting (wadding)

Sewing machine

Matching sewing thread

Masking tape

Take ½ in (1.5 cm) seam allowances throughout unless otherwise stated.

3. Cut a piece of fabric on the bias 40 in (100 cm) long and 1½ in (4 cm) wide. (Join several pieces together if necessary.) With right sides together, pin it all around the right side of the mat, aligning the raw edges. Fold under the end for a neat finish and machine stitch in place. Trim the corners.

4. To make the hanging loop, cut a 7 x 2 in (18 x 5 cm) strip of patterned fabric. Fold over the long edges by ³⁄₈ in (1 cm) and then fold in half lengthwise. Machine stitch, stitching as close to the edge as possible. Fold the bias strip over to the back of the mat and turn under ³⁄₈ in (1 cm). Pin, then slipstitch to the mat all the way around, centering the loop on one side.

Place mat and napkin

Add a touch of elegance to your dinner table with these smart place mats and matching napkins. Quick and easy to make, they would be an ideal wedding or housewarming gift that the recipients will treasure for many years to come.

As table linen requires regular laundering, make sure you wash all the fabrics before you start sewing so that there's no risk of them shrinking once the project is finished.

Placemat: 1 hour

Napkin: 20 minutes

YOU WILL NEED

For each place mat:

20 in (50 cm) patterned fabric

20 in (50 cm) gingham fabric

20 in (50 cm) plain fabric

20 in (50 cm) medium-weight iron-on interfacing

For each napkin:

20 in (50 cm) patterned fabric

20 in (50 cm) gingham fabric

Sewing machine

Needle and matching sewing thread

Take ½ in (1.5 cm) seam allowances throughout unless otherwise stated.

TO MAKE THE PLACE MATS

1. For each place mat, cut a 13½ x 10 in (34 x 26 cm) rectangle of plain fabric, two 13½ x 4½ in (34 x 12 cm) rectangles of patterned fabric, and two 13½ x 2¼ in (34 x 6 cm) rectangles of gingham fabric. With right sides together, machine stitch one gingham piece along each long side of the plain fabric, then machine stitch one patterned piece to the other long side of each gingham piece. Press the seams open.

2. Cut a 13½ x 19½ in (34 x 50 cm) piece of interfacing. Lay the interfacing on the wrong side of the fabric panel, with the rough side down. Place a damp cloth on top and iron with a medium iron to fuse the interfacing to the fabric.

3. For the backing, cut a piece of gingham and a piece of interfacing, each measuring 13½ x 19½ in (34 x 50 cm). Iron the interfacing to the reverse of the gingham, as before. Lay the front of the mat right side up on your work surface with the back piece on top, right side down. Machine stitch all around the edge, leaving a gap of about 4 in (10 cm) in one side. Trim the corners. Turn right side out and hand stitch the opening closed. Press. Machine topstitch all around the edges.

TO MAKE THE NAPKINS

For each napkin, cut a 16 in (40 cm) square of patterned fabric and a 16 in (40 cm) square of gingham fabric. With right sides together, machine stitch all around, leaving a gap of about 4 in (10 cm) in one side. Trim the corners. Turn right side out and hand stitch the opening closed. Press. Machine topstitch all around the edges, 1 in (2.5 cm) from the edge.

Napkin ring with button detail

Scraps of leftover fabric can be put to brilliant use in these charming napkin rings. The ends of each ring are stitched together and decorated with a single button—a great way of adding a pretty little finishing detail without having to go to the bother of stitching a buttonhole.

45 minutes

YOU WILL NEED

10 in (25 cm) patterned fabric

10 in (25 cm) plain fabric

20 in (50 cm) ricrac braid

20 in (50 cm) narrow gingham ribbon

Sewing machine

Needle and matching sewing thread

Button approx. ¾ in (2 cm) in diameter

Take ½ in (1.5 cm) seam allowances throughout unless otherwise stated.

1. For each napkin ring, cut a 1½ x 9 in (4 x 23 cm) rectangle of patterned fabric and two 3¼ x 9 in (8.5 x 23 cm) rectangles of plain fabric. Center the patterned fabric on top of one of the plain pieces and baste (tack) in place (see page 119).

2. Baste (tack) and then machine stitch one length of ricrac braid along each long edge of the patterned fabric. Baste and then machine stitch one length of ribbon over the edge of each length of ricrac, leaving half the ricrac visible. Remove all the basting stitches.

3. With right sides together, pin and baste (tack) the decorated strip of fabric and the remaining plain piece together. Machine stitch along three sides, leaving one short end open. Remove the basting stitches. Trim the seam allowance, turn right side out, and press. Fold in the open end of the napkin ring by ½ in (1.5 cm) and slipstitch closed (see page 119).

4. Overlap the short ends of the strip by about 1 in (2.5 cm) and stitch a button in place, stitching through all layers.

Fringed tablecloth with braid

This fabulously floral tablecloth is extremely easy to make—and will add a burst of color to any room. Simply stitch a fringed braid around a hemmed square of fabric and add a pretty ribbon with little bows to finish.

1½ hours

YOU WILL NEED

Floral fabric

Cotton fringing

Thin ribbon

Sewing machine and matching sewing thread

Take ½ in (1.5 cm) seam allowances throughout unless otherwise stated.

1. Cut a piece of floral fabric to fit your table, adding about 12 in (30 cm) on all sides for the overhang and 1 in (2.5 cm) for the hem. Fold over ⅜ in (1 cm) and another ½ in (1.5 cm) to the wrong side all the way around. Pin and machine stitch in place. Press.

2. Pin the fringing all the way around the edge of the fabric and machine stitch it in place, folding the end under for a neat finish.

3. Pin and machine stitch the ribbon along the top of the fringing, again folding the end under slightly. Tie eight small ribbon bows. Hand stitch one to each corner and one centrally along each side.

Table runner

A table runner can add the finishing touch to a dinner table. This easy-to-stitch runner is made from a bold, modern fabric and will work equally well laid on top of a plain-colored tablecloth or straight onto the table for a more informal look. If there is no obvious lengthwise pattern, you can economize on fabric by cutting the fabric across the width, joining two widths together to make a long strip if necessary.

| 1½ hours |

YOU WILL NEED

Patterned fabric

Plain fabric

Sewing machine and matching sewing thread

Needle and thread

6 self-cover buttons 2 in (5 cm) in diameter

Take ½ in (1.5 cm) seam allowances throughout unless otherwise stated.

1. Decide how long you want the runner to be. Cut two pieces of patterned fabric 1¼ in (3 cm) longer than this measurement and 13 in (33 cm) wide.

2. Cut two pieces of plain fabric the same length as the patterned fabric and 4 in (11 cm) wide. With right sides together, pin and machine stitch one plain piece along each side of one of the patterned pieces. Press the seams open.

3. With right sides together, pin and machine stitch the second piece of patterned fabric to the remaining raw edges of the plain fabric pieces to form a tube. Carefully press the seams open.

4. Pin across the short ends of the runner, making sure that the seams of the patterned fabrics align and that you have an even-sized border of plain fabric on each side. Machine stitch along one short end of the runner and turn right side out.

5. Turn under ½ in (1.5 cm) on the open end of the runner and hand stitch closed. Press carefully.

6. Following the manufacturer's instructions, cover the buttons with patterned fabric. Hand stitch three buttons to each end of the runner, spacing them evenly across the patterned fabric.

Recipe book cover

Keep all your recipes together in this pretty but practical book. I used fabric with an old-fashioned feel and maintained the nostalgic theme by using a vintage button and ties to hold everything in place, while a ribbon stitched into the lining makes a handy bookmarker.

WORKING OUT FABRIC QUANTITIES

To work out the depth of each fabric strip, measure from the top to the bottom of the book that you want to cover, add 1½ in (4 cm), and divide by three. To work out the length of each fabric strip, measure across the back, spine, and front of the book and add 6 in (15 cm).

YOU WILL NEED

Notebook

10 in (25 cm) of three floral fabrics

10 in (25 cm) gingham fabric for the lining

10 in (25 cm) medium-weight iron-on interfacing

Sewing machine and matching sewing thread

Length of ½ in (12 mm) ribbon for bookmark

12 in (30 cm) length of ⅝ in (15 mm) ribbon for ties

Square button 1 in (2.5 cm) in diameter

Take ½ in (1.5 cm) seam allowances throughout unless otherwise stated.

1. Cut three strips of floral fabric to the required size. With right sides together, pin and machine stitch the strips together. Press the seams open.

2. Cut a piece of gingham fabric and a piece of interfacing the same size as the floral piece. Using a damp cloth, iron the interfacing to the back of the gingham.

3. Place the floral piece right side up on your work surface. For the bookmark, cut a piece of narrow ribbon 2 in (5 cm) longer than the book and pin it centrally along one long edge. Place the lining piece wrong side up on top. Pin and machine stitch together, leaving an opening of about 3 in (7 cm) along one side. Trim the corners, turn right side out, and press. Hand stitch the opening closed.

4. Fold over the side edges by 2¼ in (5.5 cm) and pin. Check that the cover fits the notebook snugly. Topstitch all around. Cut two 6 in (15 cm) lengths of ⅝ in (15 mm) ribbon for the ties. Stitch one to the front of the book and one to the back and finish with a button on the front, making sure that you only stitch through the top layer of the cover.

CHAPTER 3

Bedrooms

Reversible duvet cover

Choose bold, contemporary fabrics for this reversible duvet cover. It can be difficult to buy fabric that is wide enough to fit a double bed, especially if you're using a fabric with a large pattern, so joining squares of fabric together is the perfect solution. The backing is made from two lengths of fabric stitched together to make the required width.

3 hours

1. Cut eight 20¾ in (53 cm) squares of each of the two patterned fabrics.

YOU WILL NEED

90 in (225 cm) each of 2 coordinating patterned fabrics

180 in (450 cm) striped fabric

Sewing machine and matching sewing thread

Take ½ in (1.5 cm) seam allowances throughout unless otherwise stated.

2. With right sides together, alternating the fabrics, pin and machine stitch the squares together to form four rows of four squares each. Press the seams open.

3. With right sides together, pin and machine stitch the four patchwork rows together to make a block of 16 squares. Press the seams open.

4. Cut two pieces of striped fabric 80 in (203 cm) long and the full width of the fabric. Cut off one of the selvages on each piece. With right sides together, pin and machine stitch the pieces together along the cut edges. Press the seam open. Place the fabric on your work surface. Measure 40 in (101.5 cm) either side of the center seam and use tailor's chalk to draw a line the full length of the fabric. Cut the fabric along these lines to a width of 80 in (203 cm).

5. Measure 28 in (71.5 cm) from one corner of the patchwork panel and make a cut ½ in (1.5 cm) deep. Repeat from the other corner of the same edge of the panel. Press the central section to the wrong side by ¼ in (5 mm) and then turn this over by another ⅜ in (1 cm). Pin and machine stitch along the folded-over section. Repeat on the striped panel of fabric.

6. With right sides together, pin the front of the duvet cover to the back piece. Machine stitch from the stitched section at the bottom all the way around to the other end of the stitched section.

7. Snip the corners of the seam allowance off, turn right side out, and press.

Sheet with ribbon trim

There is nothing more inviting than fresh, cotton bed linen. Embroidered and hand-decorated linens can be expensive, so cheat by sewing pretty ribbons along the top edge of a store-bought sheet. Stitch ribbons onto pillowcases to complete the look, using colors that coordinate with the décor of the room.

45 minutes

YOU WILL NEED

White sheet

Three coordinating lengths of ribbon ⅜ in (1 cm), ½ in (1.5 cm), and 1¼ in (3 cm) in width

Sewing machine and matching sewing thread

1. Measure the sheet and cut a length of ½ in (1.5 cm) ribbon about 2 in (5 cm) longer than the width of the sheet. Pin the ribbon along the top of the sheet ½ in (1.5 cm) from the edge, folding under 1 in (2.5 cm) at each end. Measure from the edge of the sheet to the ribbon as you work to ensure that it's straight. Machine stitch in place.

2. Following Step 1, cut a length of the 1¼ in (3 cm) ribbon, pin it across the sheet ¼ in (5 mm) below the first, and machine stitch in place.

3. Pin the narrowest ribbon across the sheet, ½ in (1.5 cm) below the second ribbon, and machine stitch as before.

Pillow slip with patterned border

Make crisp, white cotton pillowcases even more appealing by adding a decorative fabric border. You could use the same fabric to edge sheets, as well—a simple way to create a really special wedding or housewarming gift.

YOU WILL NEED

30 in (75 cm) patterned fabric

10 in (25 cm) plain fabric

20 in (50 cm) of
¼ in (5 mm) ribbon

50 in (125 cm) white fabric

Sewing machine

Matching sewing thread

Needle

Take ½ in (1.5 cm) seam allowances throughout unless otherwise stated.

1. Cut a 21 x 16 in (53 x 41 cm) piece of patterned fabric and two 21 x 3 in (53 x 7 cm) pieces of plain fabric. With right sides together, aligning the raw edges, lay one plain strip along each long side of the patterned fabric. Pin and machine stitch in place. Press the seams open. Pin and stitch the ribbon over one of the seams.

2. Cut a 21 x 21¼ in (53 x 54 cm) piece of white fabric. With right sides together, pin and stitch the border piece onto the white fabric, with the ribbon-edged plain piece closest to this seam. Press the seam towards the border piece.

3. At the other end of the border, fold over ½ in (1.5 cm) to the wrong side and press. With wrong sides together, fold the border back on itself and hand stitch in place, aligning the folded edge with the edge of the border on the front. Press.

4. Cut a 21 x 38½ in (53 x 98 cm) piece of white fabric. Along one short end, fold over ⅜ in (1 cm) and then another ½ in (1.5 cm). Machine stitch, stitching as close to the edge as possible. Lay the piece right side up on your work surface. Lay the front of the cover right side down on top, aligning the raw edges. Fold the hemmed flap of white fabric over the front of the cover. Pin and machine stitch along the short raw end and both long sides. Trim the seams and turn right side out. Press.

Patchwork bedspread

This colorful patchwork quilt, made from pretty floral and polka-dot fabrics, uses large, machine-sewn squares of fabric—a time-saving way to create a bedspread with a homespun feel. Remember, when you're making patchwork it's important to use fabrics of similar weights.

For this design, choose fabrics with similar colors, adding a few contrasting patterns for a fresh, modern look. Finish off the quilt with a ribbon border and stitch on an assortment of buttons which, as well as providing a decorative touch, hold the layers of the quilt together.

YOU WILL NEED

20 in (50 cm) each of six cotton fabrics

Pattern paper

60 in (150 cm) backing fabric

60 in (150 cm) lightweight batting (wadding)

Sewing machine

Needle and matching sewing threads

192 in (490 cm) length of ribbon

Assorted buttons

Take ½ in (1.5 cm) seam allowances throughout unless otherwise stated.

1. Cut a 7½ in (19 cm) square piece of paper to use as a pattern. Cut out squares from a range of different fabrics by folding the fabrics over concertina style and laying the pattern piece on top, so that you can cut squares from several layers at once. You will need 54 squares in total.

2. Lay the fabric squares out on your work surface in six rows of nine squares each and move them around until you have a pleasing arrangement, making sure that no two squares of the same fabric are next to each other. Pin a paper label onto each row of squares, numbered from 1 to 9.

3. Starting with row 1, pin and machine stitch the squares together. Press open the seams. Repeat with the remaining eight rows of squares.

4. Lay the strips on your work surface in the correct order. Pin and machine stitch them together, aligning the seams, and press the seams open. Remove the paper labels.

5. Lay the backing fabric on your work surface, with the batting (wadding) on top and the patchwork panel on top of the batting. Pin all the layers together and cut the batting and backing to the same size as the patchwork. Remove the pins.

6. Place the backing fabric to one side. Pin and baste (tack) the patchwork panel to the batting (wadding). Work from the center outwards, pinning in a diagonal line out to each corner, and then in a straight line from the center to the center of each side.

7. Lay the patchwork and batting (wadding) panel right side up on your work surface, with the backing fabric right side down on top. Pin through all layers, working from the center outwards as in Step 6. Machine stitch, leaving a 12 in (30 cm) opening at one end. Snip the corners and trim the seam allowance a little.

8. Turn the quilt right side out and press. Hand stitch the opening closed. Pin, baste (tack), and machine stitch the ribbon onto the top of the quilt, about ½ in (1.5 cm) in from the edge all the way around. Miter the corners for a neat finish. Turn the end of the ribbon under a little and stitch to finish.

9. Hand stitch buttons onto the quilt, making sure that the stitches go through all layers of the quilt. Use a selection of buttons in a random arrangement.

Sheer drape with ribbons

2½ hours

With so many lovely patterned sheer fabrics in the shops now, it is easy to make something practical that still makes a statement in a room. Here, I've used lengths of ribbons and braids to make a pretty border.

YOU WILL NEED

Sheer fabric

5 different ribbons and ricrac braid the width of the finished drape (curtain) plus 4 in (10 cm)

Sewing machine and matching sewing thread

1. Cut a piece of sheer fabric to the required size (see right). Arrange the ribbons and ricrac braid across the bottom of the fabric, leaving at least 1½ in (4 cm) below the first ribbon to allow for the hem. Pin, baste (tack), and machine stitch the ribbons and braid in place, and then trim the ends level with the edge of the fabric.

> **WORKING OUT FABRIC QUANTITIES**
>
> If the drape (curtain) is to be pulled fairly taut on the pole, you will need to cut a piece of fabric that is 2 in (5 cm) wider and 2 in (5 cm) longer than the window. If you want the drape to be slightly gathered, allow about 25% extra when calculating the width.

2. Along the sides of the drape (curtain), turn over ⅜ in (1 cm) and then another ½ in (1.5 cm) to the wrong side and press. Pin and machine stitch in place.

3. Work out how many ties you will need: the first and last ties should be positioned about 1¼ in (3 cm) from each side of the drape (curtain) and the remainder should be spaced about 6½ in (16 cm) apart. For each pair of ties, cut a 17 x 5 in (43 x 13 cm) piece of fabric. With right sides together, fold each piece of fabric in half and machine stitch along the length and across one short end. Turn right side out, press the raw end under by ½ in (1.5 cm) and hand stitch closed. Fold the ties in half and pin to the top of the right side of the drape. Cut a piece of fabric the same width as the drape and 3 in (8 cm) deep. With right sides together, pin it along the top of the drape. Machine stitch in place.

4. Fold the fabric strip over to the wrong side of the drape (curtain) and press ½ in (1.5 cm) under along the remaining raw edges. Machine stitch the strip to the back of the drape. At the bottom of the drape, turn under ⅜ in (1 cm) and then another ½ in (1.5 cm) and machine stitch in place. Press.

CHAPTER 4

Work and play spaces

Drawstring toy bags

2 hours

You can never have enough storage space for toys and these drawstring bags are both functional and pretty. Made from oddments of fabric sewn together and decorated with a cute fabric flower, you can simply throw toys in them at the end of the day and hang on a peg rail. They would work equally well for storing a gym kit or ballet shoes.

YOU WILL NEED

10 in (25 cm) of three coordinating fabrics

20 in (50 cm) backing fabric

18 in (45 cm) of three coordinating ribbons

50 in (125 cm) cord

Sewing machine

Template on page 122

Needle and thread

Scraps of fabric

Button 1¼ in (3 cm) in diameter

Take ½ in (1.5 cm) seam allowances throughout unless otherwise stated.

1. Cut a 17½ x 7 in (45 x 18 cm) piece of each of the three coordinating fabrics. With right sides together, machine stitch them together along their long edges. Press the seams open. Machine stitch one ribbon over each seam on the right side. Press.

2. Cut a 19 x 17½ in (48 x 45 cm) piece of fabric for the back of the bag. With right sides together, machine stitch the front and back together, leaving 2¾ in (7 cm) unstitched at the top of one side. Turn back the unstitched part of the side edges, so that it's level with the stitching, and press. Trim the corners at the base of the bag to reduce bulk. Fold the top of the bag over by ⅜ in (1 cm) and again by 1¼ in (3 cm). Machine stitch close to the folded edge to create a channel, then turn the bag right side out.

3. Cut two 8 in (21 cm) lengths of ribbon and machine stitch together to create a double thickness. Stitch onto the middle of the back of the bag, just below the channel, folding the ends under by ⅜ in (1 cm). Thread the cord through the channel. Cut two 2⅔ x 3 in (7 x 8 cm) rectangles of fabric. With wrong sides together, fold each piece in half widthwise and machine stitch along both sides. Turn right side out and turn under the top edge by ⅜ in (1 cm). Push the ends of the cord into this pocket and machine stitch along the top.

4. Using the template on page 122, cut two petal shapes from each of five different fabrics. Pin each pair together and machine stitch around the edge, leaving a small gap for turning. Turn right side out and make a few small stitches to gather at the end. Stitch the five petals together to form a flower, and hand stitch to the bag, with a button in the center. Attach the tip of each petal to the bag by making a few small stitches at the back.

Lined storage basket

This fabric lining is practical as well as pretty, as it prevents delicate items from snagging on the wicker basket. The idea could also be used to create linings for storage baskets for linens, clothing, and even toys.

WORKING OUT FABRIC QUANTITIES

To work out how much fabric you need for the sides of the basket, measure around the top of the outside of the basket and add 1¼ in (3 cm). Then measure the height and add the amount that you want to fold over to the outside of the basket, plus ½ in (1.5 cm).

To work out how much fabric you need for the base of the basket, measure along one long edge and add 1¼ in (3 cm). Then measure along one short side and add 1¼ in (3 cm) to this measurement, too.

You will also need enough ribbon to go all around the top of the basket and the handles, plus 48 in (120 cm).

YOU WILL NEED

Patterned fabric

Ribbon ½ in (15 mm) wide

Sewing machine and matching sewing thread

Basket

Take ½ in (1.5 cm) seam allowances throughout unless otherwise stated.

1. Cut a strip of patterned fabric for the sides of the basket (see above). With right sides together, pin the ends together. Place the fabric inside the basket, wrong side out. Check that it fits snugly around the top of the basket and fold it over to make sure that the lining will not be too tight. Machine stitch the ends together and press the seam open.

2. Put the lining back into the basket, wrong side out, and press it into the corners with your fingers so that it fits snugly all around. Pin and baste (tack) any excess fabric at the corners to form a neat dart. Take the lining out of the basket and machine stitch the corners. (If the sides of your basket are straight, you can omit this step.)

3. Cut a rectangle of fabric for the base of the basket. With right sides together, machine stitch the sides of the lining to the base. Trim the corners and press.

4. Place the lining inside the basket and mark where the handles are. Cut out a rectangle at each end that is exactly the same size as the handles. Take the lining out of the basket.

5. For each handle, cut a length of ribbon slightly longer than the sides and base of the handle rectangle and press it in half widthwise. Pin, baste (tack), and machine stitch the ribbon around the handle of the lining, folding the ribbon neatly at the corners.

6. Cut a length of ribbon to fit around one side of the lining plus 24 in (60 cm). Press in half widthwise and pin, baste (tack), and machine stitch it along one side of the lining leaving 12 in (30 cm) of ribbon free at each end. Repeat along the other side of the lining. Press and place the lining inside the basket, tying the ribbons with a neat bow at either end.

Door stop

This stylish door stop made from striking floral and spotted fabrics can be moved around as and when it is needed. You could simplify the design by using just one fabric and replacing the fabric handle with wide cotton ribbon.

YOU WILL NEED

10 in (25 cm) patterned fabric

10 in (25 cm) spotted fabric

30 in (75 cm) length of ¼ in (5 mm) ribbon

Thick cardboard

Dried peas

Stuffing

Sewing machine and matching sewing thread

Take ½ in (1.5 cm) seam allowances throughout unless otherwise stated.

1. Cut out two 8¼ x 6 in (21 x 15 cm) and two 7 x 6 in (18 x 15 cm) rectangles of patterned fabric. Cut two 8¼ x 3½ in (21 x 9 cm) and two 7 x 3½ in (18 x 9 cm) rectangles of spotted fabric.

2. With right sides together, pin and machine stitch a spotted rectangle to a patterned rectangle of the same width, until you have four panels. (These will form the sides of the door stop.) Press the seams open.

3. Pin and machine stitch a length of ribbon over the seam on all four panels of fabric.

4. For the top and bottom of the door stop, cut an 8¼ x 7 in (21 x 18 cm) rectangle of each fabric.

5. Cut a 10 x 4¼ in (25 x 11 cm) strip of patterned fabric for the handle. With right sides together, fold the strip in half lengthwise, then pin and machine stitch along the longest edge. Turn right side out and press. Pin the handle centrally across the fabric for the top of the door stop, turning under the ends. At each end, machine stitch a rectangle about 2¼ in (5.5 cm) long to attach the handle firmly.

6. With right sides together, pin and machine stitch the four side panels together, alternating the sizes of the panels, to form a loop. Press the seams open.

7. With right sides together, pin and machine stitch the top of the door stop to the side piece. Snip the corners. Pin and stitch the bottom piece to the bottom of the sides in the same way, leaving one short side open. Turn right side out and press.

8. Cut two 7 x 6 in (18 x 15 cm) pieces of card and push them inside the fabric box, one at the bottom and one at the top. Half fill the box with stuffing and then pour in dried peas until the box is fairly solid. Hand stitch the open side closed.

Sewing kit

3 hours

With this neat little sewing kit, all your needles, pins, thread, and buttons can be kept just where you need them. Made from a bold spotted fabric and lined with felt, it can be adapted to hold all kinds of things, from sewing and knitting accessories to stationery and art equipment, and is easily portable, too.

YOU WILL NEED

20 in (50 cm) red felt

20 in (50 cm) spotted fabric

20 in (50 cm) medium-weight iron-on interfacing

Sewing machine and matching sewing thread

Large press stud

Large button

Sewing items for the kit—embroidery threads, needles, pins, tape measure, buttons, tailor's chalk, etc.

Take ½ in (1.5 cm) seam allowances throughout unless otherwise stated.

1. Using pinking shears, cut a 16½ x9½ in (42 x 24 cm). rectangle of red felt. Press with a warm iron. Measure 4 in (10 cm) in from each short end and mark with pins to show where the folds will be.

2. Lay the felt on your work surface and arrange the contents of the sewing kit on it, avoiding the fold lines. Cut rectangles of spotted fabric ¾ in (2 cm) wide and as long as necessary to hold the items in place, adding 1¼ in (3 cm) all around each piece. Fold under ½ in (1.5 cm) all the way around each rectangle and press. Using pinking shears, cut rectangles of felt ¼ in (5 mm) bigger all the way round than the fabric rectangles. Machine stitch the fabric rectangles onto the felt pieces.

3. Machine stitch the felt-backed spotted rectangles onto the large felt piece in the required positions. Stitch a 12 in (30 cm) length of ribbon onto the felt to hold the tape measure in place.

4. Cut two 12 x 18¾ in (30 x 47.5 cm) pieces of spotted fabric. Cut two pieces of interfacing the same size. Lay one piece of interfacing on the back of each piece of spotted fabric, rough side down. Place a damp cloth on top and iron with a medium iron to fuse the interfacing to the fabric. Center the felt panel on the right side of one of the spotted pieces.

5. Cut two 2¾ in (7 cm) squares of spotted fabric for the tab. With right sides together, pin and stitch around three sides of the fabric. Trim the seam allowance to ¼ in (5 mm), turn right side out, and press.

6. Using pinking shears, cut a piece of red felt ¼ in (5 mm) bigger all around than the tab. Center the tab on the felt and machine stitch in place.

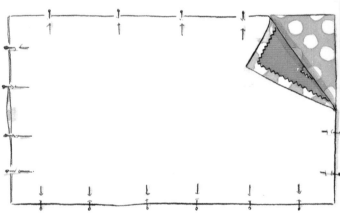

7. With right sides together, pin the front and back of the folder together. Place the tab in the center of one short side, aligning the raw edge of the spotted fabric with the raw edge of the front. Machine stitch all the way around, leaving an opening of about 3 in (8 cm) in one side. Trim the corners, turn right side out, and press.

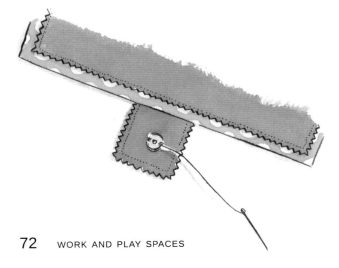

8. Hand stitch the opening closed. Sew half of the press stud onto the inside of the tab and stitch the other half onto the front of the folder.

9. Stitch the button securely onto the front of the tab. Press the folder and then fill it with the sewing kit.

Fabric-covered storage box

This is a great storage solution for a home office. Make a whole range in different sizes to keep stationery or correspondence close at hand.

WORKING OUT FABRIC QUANTITIES

Decide how tall and wide you want the box to be. Add the measurements for all four sides together, and then add 1¼ in (3 cm). Add 1¼ in (3 cm) to the height of the box. Take the measurement for the box base and add 1¼ in (3 cm) to both the width and the length.

1. To make the handle, cut a 6 x 3 in (15 x 7.5 cm) rectangle of fabric 1. Fold it in half lengthwise, pin, and machine stitch along the long raw edge. Turn right side out and press. Fold the ends under by ½ in (1.5 cm) and press.

2. Measure ½ in (1.5 cm) from one end of the strip of fabric for the sides of the box and mark with a pin. Measure the width of the box from this mark. Pin on the handle at this point and machine stitch a square at the end. Pin the other end in place and machine stitch in place.

3. With right sides together, pin and machine stitch the short ends of the strip together. Press the seam open.

4. With right sides together, pin and machine stitch the side piece to the base, making sure that the handle is positioned centrally along one short side.

5. Snip the corners and press all the seams open.

6. Cut out the lining from your coordinating fabric, using the same measurements as before. With right sides together, pin and machine stitch the short ends of the strip together and press the seam open. With right sides together, pin and machine stitch the side strip to the base, leaving one short side open. Snip the corners and press the seams open.

7. With right sides together, pin and machine stitch the two fabric box shapes together, leaving one short end open. Press the seam open and turn right side out. Form a box shape with the lining on the inside.

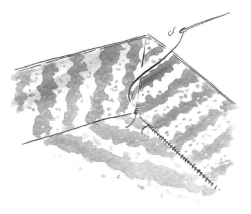

8. Cut out a rectangle of cardboard to fit the base of the box. insert it into the base of the box through the unstitched opening. Measure and cut two pieces of cardboard for the long sides and two for the short sides. Slot the longer pieces into the sides of the fabric box and the shorter lengths into the ends.

9. Hand stitch the open end closed. Make a few small stitches at each corner through all the layers to hold the lining in place.

Floor pillow

1 hour

Make a pile of these comfy floor pillows to sink into with a good book or to provide extra seating when guests come to visit. Use two different fabrics for each pillow and cover the button at the center of each pillow with a coordinating fabric for extra interest. The covers cannot be taken off without removing the buttons, so make sure you use pillow forms (pads) that are machine washable so that you can throw the whole thing into the machine for easy cleaning.

YOU WILL NEED

30 in (75 cm) each of two coordinating fabrics

Pillow form (pad) 25½ in (65 cm) square

2 self-cover buttons 1¼ in (3 cm) in diameter

Sewing machine

Needle

Matching sewing thread

Upholstery thread and needle

Take ½ in (1.5 cm) seam allowances throughout unless otherwise stated.

1. Cut a 26¾ in (68 cm) square of each fabric. Lay one square right side up on your work surface and place the second one right side down on top of it, aligning all edges. Pin and machine stitch all around, leaving a gap of about 12 in (30 cm) in one side. Trim the corners close to the stitching to reduce the bulk.

2. Turn the cover right side out and press. insert the pillow form (pad) and hand stitch the opening closed, using small stitches. Find the center point of the pillow cover on both sides and mark with a pin.

3. Following the manufacturer's instructions, cover the buttons with fabric. Thread an upholstery needle and knot the thread. Stitch through the pillow at the central pin and thread on a button. Take the needle back through the pillow and thread a button onto the other side. Pull the thread firmly to pull the buttons into the pillow. Stitch back through the buttons a couple of times and secure with a few stitches.

Roll-up blind

2 hours

Patterned fabric

Coordinating gingham fabric

Sewing machine and matching sewing thread

Dowelling ½ in (15 mm) in diameter

Two metal rings 1½ in (4 cm) in diameter

Length of 2 x 1 in (5 x 2.5 mm) wood

Hook-and-loop tape (Velcro)

Fast-drying craft glue

½ in (12 mm) ribbon

Take ½ in (1.5 cm) seam allowances throughout unless otherwise stated.

This simple blind, made from a bold floral fabric backed with a coordinating gingham check, can be made very quickly. As the blind has to be rolled up manually, it is ideal for rooms where it can be kept raised most of the time. Ribbons tied in pretty bows hold the blind in place when raised. The wooden dowelling in the bottom of the panel ensures that the blind forms a neat roll and does not sag.

1. Cut a piece of patterned fabric and a piece of gingham fabric 1¼ in (3 cm) wider and 2¾ in (7 cm) longer than the finished blind. With right sides together, pin and machine stitch them together along both sides and the bottom. Snip off the corners.

2. Turn right side out and press. Cut a piece of dowelling to fit the width of the panel and push it down inside the blind. Hand stitch just above the dowelling to keep it in place.

3. Make two tabs to hold the metal rings. Cut two 3½ x 9 in (9 x 23 cm) rectangles of patterned fabric. With right sides together, fold them in half lengthwise and machine stitch ½ in (1.5 cm) from the edge. Turn right side out and press, with the seam in the middle of the tab. Thread each tab through a ring and fold in half.

4. Fold the open end of the blind over to the wrong side by ½ in (1.5 cm) and again by 1½ in (4 cm), placing the tabs under the hem 7 in (17 cm) in from each side. Machine stitch along the bottom of the folded panel.

5. Cut a piece of wood the same width as the blind. Cut a piece of patterned fabric 5 in (13 cm) deeper and 1½ in (4 cm) wider than the wood. Center the wood on the fabric and glue it in place, folding the corners of the fabric in neatly.

6. Cut a piece of hook-and-loop tape (Velcro) the same length as the wood and glue one half of it onto the wood. Screw the wood into the window frame.

7. Cut two pieces of ribbon the same length as the blind. Pin and machine stitch the other half of the hook-and-loop tape to the top of the blind on the wrong side, placing one length of ribbon 7 in (17 cm) in from each side, under the hem.

8. Roll up the blind from the bottom and stick it onto the hoop-and-loop taped (Velcroed) wood. Cut two 10 in (25 cm) lengths of ribbon ½ in (12mm wide ribbon and hand stitch one onto each ring. Bring the ribbon from the back of the blind to the front and tie to the shorter length of ribbon at the ring.

CHAPTER 5

Laundry and bathrooms

Ironing board cover

Even purely functional items such as ironing board covers don't have to be dull! Use a favorite fabric to make a padded cover that is held in place with a drawstring, making it easy to remove and wash. Thick cotton fabrics work best for this project, lined with cotton batting (wadding) that will withstand some heat.

1½ hours

YOU WILL NEED

30 in (75 cm) plain white cotton fabric

Pencil or fabric marker

30 in (75 cm) patterned fabric

30 in (75 cm) lightweight cotton batting (wadding)

Sewing machine and matching sewing thread

Approx. 79 in (2 m) white ribbon

Take ½ in (1.5 cm) seam allowances throughout unless otherwise stated.

1. Lay the ironing board on the white fabric and draw around it, adding 4 in (10 cm) all around. Cut out. Cut a piece of patterned fabric and a piece of cotton batting (wadding) to the same size.

2. Lay the patterned fabric right side up on your work surface. Place the white cotton on top, with the batting (wadding) on top of the cotton. Pin and machine stitch through all the layers, leaving an opening of about 6 in (15 cm) at the straight end. Snip the seam allowance off at the corners and trim the seam allowance to ¼ in (5 mm) all the way around.

3. Turn the cover right side out and press. Measure and machine stitch a line 2 in (5 cm) in from the edge all the way around.

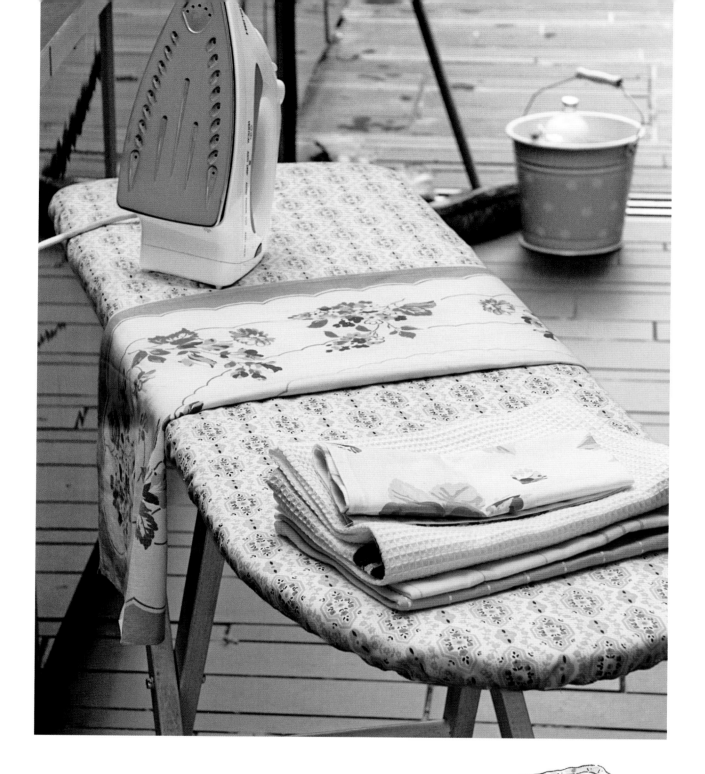

4. Attach a safety pin to the end of the ribbon and thread it through the channel all the way around the cover. Pull the ribbon to gather the cover over the ironing board and secure with a bow.

Towel with fabric border

Transform plain towels with an attractively patterned fabric border. The neat little hanging loop is a professional-looking finishing touch and means that they can be displayed on a peg rail or door hook when not in use, adding a splash of color and pattern to your bathroom. Make a set of bath and hand towels for a personal and unique gift, choosing fabrics in colors that tone in with the recipient's bathroom.

YOU WILL NEED

27 x 49 in (68 x 125 cm)
white bath towel

20 in (50 cm) patterned fabric

20 in (50 cm) gingham fabric

Sewing machine

Needle and matching
sewing thread

Take ½ in (1.5 cm) seam
allowances throughout unless
otherwise stated.

3 hours

1. Cut a 28 x 9½ in (71 x 24 cm) piece of patterned fabric, a 28 x 10½ in (71 x 27 cm) piece of gingham fabric, and a 28 x 2¼ in (71 x 6 cm) piece of gingham fabric. With right sides together, pin and machine stitch one gingham piece along each long edge of the patterned fabric. Press the seams open.

2. To make the fabric hanging loop, cut a 7½ x 2 in (19 x 5 cm) piece of patterned fabric. With wrong sides together, fold in half lengthwise and press. Open out and fold both long edges in to the central fold. Press. Fold in half again, aligning the folded edges. Pin, then machine stitch close to the edge. Press.

3. Lay the towel on your work surface, with the fabric border right side down on top of it 8½ in (22.5 cm) from one short edge of the towel. Place the fabric loop under this about 1¼ in (3 cm) on either side of the middle of the towel (widthwise), with the two raw ends sticking out. Pin, baste (tack), and machine stitch in place.

4. Fold the fabric border down over the towel and up over itself, with right sides together. Fold over ½ in (1.5 cm) along the top edge of the border and line it up with the border stitched to the towel. Machine stitch along both sides of the towel and trim the seams. Turn right side out, tucking in the end of the towel. Slipstitch the remaining border edge in place.

Drawstring laundry bag

Practical and stylish, this pretty laundry bag looks great in both the bathroom or bedroom, as well as providing a roomy and functional place to store worn clothes that are awaiting washing. The neat fabric loop means that it can be hung on the back of a door, while the drawstring close makes for easy, everyday use.

YOU WILL NEED

20 in (50 cm) patterned fabric

40 in (1 m) spotty fabric

40 in (1 m) coordinating fabric for the lining

40 in (1 m) medium-weight iron-on interfacing

Sewing machine

Matching sewing thread

Paper for pattern

Take ½ in (1.5 cm) seam allowances throughout unless otherwise stated.

3 hours

1. Cut a 40 x 10 in (102 x 25 cm) rectangle of patterned fabric and two 40 x 8 in (102 x 20 cm) rectangles of spotty fabric. Lay the patterned piece right side up on your work surface, with one of the spotty pieces right side down on top, aligning along one long raw edge. Pin, baste (tack), and machine stitch together.

2. Pin, baste (tack), and machine stitch the other spotty piece along the other raw edge. Open out both seams and press.

3. Cut a 40 x 25½ in (102 x 65 cm) piece of interfacing. Lay the interfacing on the wrong side of the fabric panel, with the rough side down. Place a damp cloth on top and iron with a medium iron to fuse the interfacing to the fabric.

4. With right sides together, pin, baste (tack), and machine stitch the side edges together, leaving a ¾ in (2 cm) opening 3¾ in (9.5 cm) from the top edge.

5. Draw a circle 13 in (33.5 cm) in diameter on paper and cut out to make a template for the base of the bag. Pin the template to the spotty fabric, draw around it, and cut out. Cut a piece of interfacing the same size and iron to the reverse of the spotty fabric, as before. With right sides together, pin, baste (tack), and machine stitch the base to the sides of the bag. Make small snips all the way around the seam allowance.

6. Cut a 40 x 19 in (102 x 48.5 cm) rectangle of fabric for the lining. Pin, baste (tack), and machine stitch along the short sides to form a tube. Press the seam open. Cut a circle of fabric and a circle of interfacing, as for the base of the bag, and iron together as before. Pin, baste, and machine stitch the base onto the lining, again making small snips around the seam allowance.

7. With wrong sides together, place the lining inside the bag. Fold over and press ½ in (1.5 cm) and then another 2 in (5 cm) around the top of the bag. Machine stitch as close as possible to the edge, and then work another line of stitching ¾ in (2 cm) below that, to form a channel.

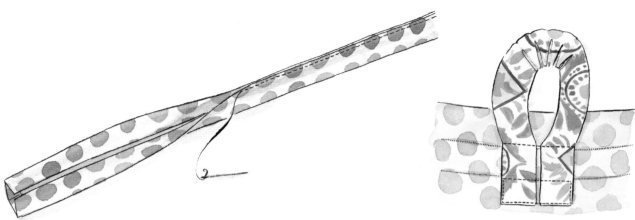

8. Cut a 55 x 2 in (140 x 5 cm) strip of fabric. Fold in half lengthwise. Open out, fold in ⅜ in (1 cm) along each long side, and press. Fold the strip in half again and stitch along it to make the drawstring.

9. Thread the drawstring through the channel at the top of the bag and tie with a knot. Cut a 9 x 2 in (23 x 5 cm) piece of fabric. Fold in half, right sides together, and machine stitch along the two long edges. Turn right side out and turn the raw ends under by ½ in (1.5 cm). Stitch onto the bag to form a loop, stitching it onto the bag above and below the drawstring channel.

Peg bag

This charming bag is the perfect place to store wooden clothes pegs and will brighten up any wash day. I used a vintage-style floral fabric topped off with a coordinating ribbon and ricrac braid, with a bright gingham lining just visible around the opening. A child's wooden hanger is the perfect size to use inside the bag, so that you can hang it on a hook in the kitchen or utility room when not in use or on the washing line when you are pegging out the laundry.

YOU WILL NEED

Templates on page 122

Tracing paper and pencil

Pattern paper

20 in (50 cm) floral fabric

20 in (50 cm) gingham fabric

20 in (50 cm) pink grosgrain ribbon, ⅜ in (1 cm) wide

20 in (50 cm) blue ricrac braid

Sewing machine and matching sewing threads

Take ½ in (1.5 cm) seam allowances throughout unless otherwise stated.

1. Use the templates on page 122 to make paper patterns (see page 119). Cut one back piece and one top and one bottom front piece from floral fabric. Repeat using the gingham fabric. Right sides together, pin and then machine stitch the floral and gingham top pieces together along the curve. Trim the seam allowance, turn right side out, and press.

2. Lay the gingham bottom front piece right side up on your work surface. Place the top front piece right side up on top of it and the floral bottom front piece wrong side up on top of that. Machine stitch along the top edge, stitching through all layers.

3. Turn right side out and press. Pin a length of blue ricrac braid across the bag about ½ in (1.5 cm) from the top of the base, with a length of pink grosgrain ribbon about ⅜ in (1 cm) below that, and machine stitch in place.

4. Lay the front of the bag right side up on your work surface, with the floral back piece right side down on top of it. Place the gingham back piece right side up on top. Machine stitch all around the edge, leaving a gap of about ¾ in (2 cm) in the center top. Turn right side out. insert the coat hanger, and stitch a grosgrain ribbon bow below the hook.

Ribbon and button lavender bag

1½ hours

Lavender has been used for centuries to freshen and scent linens, and these lovely bags can easily be slipped into drawers and linen cupboards to add a gentle fragrance. They are an effective way of using up small scraps of fabric and are finished beautifully with oddments of ribbon, braid, and pretty little vintage buttons.

YOU WILL NEED

10 in (25 cm) each of two coordinating fabrics

10 in (25 cm) each of two coordinating ribbons

10 in (25 cm) ricrac braid

Sewing machine

Needle and matching sewing thread

Dried lavender

Small funnel

Small buttons

Take ½ in (1.5 cm) seam allowances throughout unless otherwise stated.

1. Cut two 7 x 6 in (18 x 15 cm) rectangles of your main fabric and two 7 x 4¼ in (18 x 11 cm) rectangles of a coordinating fabric. With right sides together, pin and machine stitch one of each size of rectangle together. Press the seams open.

2. Cut two 7½ in (19 cm) lengths of coordinating ribbons. Pin and machine stitch one ribbon along the seam on one piece of fabric, to hide the join, and the other about ¼ in (5 mm) from the first, on the smaller section of fabric. Press.

3. Measure and cut a 27 in (69 cm) length of ricrac braid. Lay the ribbon-trimmed piece of fabric right side up on your work surface. Pin and baste (tack) the ricrac braid all the way around the edge of the fabric, easing the braid at the corners so that the center of the ricrac is exactly in line with the seam allowance.

4. With right sides together, lay the second piece of fabric on top of the first. Pin, baste (tack), and machine stitch all the way around the pieces, leaving a gap of about 2 in (5 cm) at one end. Trim the corners and trim the seams to ⅜ in (1 cm).

5. Turn the bag the right side out and gently pull the corners out for a neat finish. Press. Fill the bag with dried lavender using a small funnel. Alternatively, stuff the bag with cotton stuffing and add a little dried lavender. Hand stitch the opening closed, turning in the seam allowance. Stitch buttons onto the ribbon for extra decoration.

Padded coat hanger

Padded hangers look much prettier than plain wooden ones and are much kinder to your clothes. This hanger is made from scraps of fabric and takes no time at all to make. The flower is made from simple petal shapes hand stitched together and finishes the hanger off beautifully. Ideal as a gift, you could throw in some dried lavender before stitching the cover on to fragrance it, too.

YOU WILL NEED

Wooden coat hanger

10 in (25 cm) batting (wadding)

10 in (25 cm) main fabric

10 in (25 cm) each of three coordinating fabrics for the flower

10 in (25 cm) ribbon

Needle and thread

Button

Templates on page 123

Tracing paper, pencil, and fabric marker pen

1 hour

1. Cover the coat hanger with batting (wadding), stitching the batting securely in place, and trim off any excess. Use the templates on page 123 to make paper patterns (see page 119). Trace around the coat hanger template onto the main fabric and cut out. Turn under and press ⅜ in (1 cm) to the wrong side all around. Lay the padded coat hanger on the top half of the fabric and fold up the bottom half to cover the hanger.

2. Starting from the center and working outwards on each side, using double thread, work a row of large running stitches (see page 119) along the top of the hanger, gathering the fabric slightly as you go and securing it at the end.

3. Using the templates, cut four large flower shapes from gingham fabric. Work a small circle of running stitches in the center of each flower, then pull the thread to gather the fabric. Stitch the four shapes together at their gathered points to form one complete flower.

4. Repeat with two spotty fabrics, making the final layer smaller. Stitch all three flowers together. Stitch a red-and-white gingham ribbon bow to the center of the flower with a button.

CHAPTER 6

Outside spaces

Awning

3½ hours

YOU WILL NEED

79 in (2 m) striped fabric

60 in (150 cm) cotton tape

Sewing machine and matching sewing thread

Template on page 124

Tracing paper, pencil, and paper for pattern

Tailor's chalk

6 large buttons

Two ⅝ in (15 mm) metal eyelets

Hammer to fix the eyelets

Two lengths of ¾ in (2 cm) wooden dowelling

Two wooden finials

Approx. 3 yd (3 m) cord

Pinking shears

Bradawl

Take ½ in (1.5 cm) seam allowances throughout unless otherwise stated.

Create shade and shelter with this simple garden awning. Use heavyweight cotton or canvas and metal eyelets to make an instant garden canopy that is easy to put up and is very transportable. The awning can be tied to any sturdy structure such as fencing or trees; you could even attach it to the side of your house to create a shady patio area by fitting hooks to the wall.

1. Turn over and pin ⅜ in (1 cm) and then another ½ in (1.5 cm) on all sides of the striped fabric. Cut two 30 in (75 cm) lengths of cotton tape, fold in half, and machine stitch at two of the corners.

2. At the opposite end to the tapes, fold over 9½ in (24 cm) to the wrong side. Use the template on page 124 to make a paper pattern (see page 119). Lay the pattern on the folded-over section and draw around it with tailor's chalk, moving it along each time until there are six triangles to form a line of bunting.

3. Machine stitch along the chalk lines. Cut around the triangles with pinking shears about ¼ in (5 mm) from the stitched line.

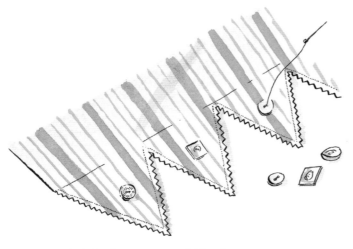

4. Hand stitch a button onto each triangle.

5. Following the manufacturer's instructions, fix an eyelet at each side of the bunting.

6. Cut the dowelling to the required length. Using a bradawl, make a hole in one end of each piece of dowelling.

7. Place a piece of dowelling on the underside of an eyelet, and screw a finial into it securely.

8. Tie the tape onto hooks screwed into a wall or to the branches of a tree. Push the ends of the dowelling into the ground, pulling the awning taut. Loop cord around the bottom of the finials, pull taut, and fasten to the ground with tent pegs.

Picnic blanket

3 hours

Bright, cheerful fabrics in various tones of sunshine yellow make this the perfect blanket for a summer picnic. Make sure that all the fabrics you choose are machine washable, so that the blanket is easy to clean, and use a heavy cotton fabric for the backing to give it some weight.

YOU WILL NEED

60 in (150 cm) patterned fabric

20 in (50 cm) each of two spotted fabrics

80 in (2 m) heavyweight gingham fabric for backing

256 in (6.5 m) grosgrain ribbon 7⁄8 in (22 mm) wide

Sewing machine and matching sewing thread

Needle and thread

Take 1⁄2 in (1.5 cm) seam allowances throughout unless otherwise stated.

1. From each spotted fabric, cut eighteen 5¾ in (15 cm) squares. To speed things up, you can make a paper pattern the right size, then fold the fabric several times, pin the pattern on top, and cut through several layers at once.

2. Alternating the fabrics, pin and machine stitch the squares together into two strips of eight squares and two strips of ten.

3. Cut a 39 in (99 cm) square of patterned fabric. With right sides together, pin and machine stitch the two eight-square strips to opposite sides of the large square. Press the seams open.

4. With right sides together, pin and machine stitch the longer strips to the two remaining sides of the square, making sure that each corner square is next to a different spotted fabric. Press the seams open.

5. Cut a 48½ in (123 cm) square of gingham fabric for the back of the blanket. With right sides together, pin and machine stitch the front and back of the blanket together, leaving an opening of about 8 in (20 cm) along one side. Trim the corners and turn right side out.

6. Press the blanket and hand stitch the opening closed.

7. Lay the blanket on your work surface and pin, baste (tack), and machine stitch grosgrain ribbon all the way round the seam between the border and the central square, turning the ribbon over at each corner for a neat finish.

8. Cut four 9 in (22 cm) lengths of grosgrain ribbon and form each one into a loop. Stitch the ends together. Cut four 2½ in (6 cm) pieces of ribbon and wrap one around the middle of each ribbon loop to form four bows, securing each one with a few stitches at the back. Stitch one bow onto each corner over the stitched ribbon.

Templates on page 125

Tracing paper, pencil, and paper for patterns

237 in (6 m) patterned fabric

237 in (6 m) fabric for lining

69 in (175 cm) ribbon
¾ in (2 cm) wide

Sewing machine and matching sewing thread

Needle and thread

78 in (4 x 2 m) lengths of ½ in (15 mm) dowelling

Take ½ in (1.5 cm) seam allowances throughout unless otherwise stated.

Children's play tent

6 hours

Children will love this play tent! Made in a traditional tepee shape, it requires moderate sewing skill and takes slightly longer to make than many of the other projects in this book— but don't be put off! It really is worth the effort and is sturdy enough to last for many years, guaranteeing hours and hours of fun for all those who are lucky enough to play in it.

1. Draw pattern templates following the dimensions given on the templates on page 125 and cut out. Pin the patterns to your chosen fabric and cut three pieces of fabric for the sides of the text and two for the front. With right sides together, pin and machine stitch the three side pieces together. Press the seams open. With right sides together, following the diagram, pin and machine stitch one front piece to each side. Press the seams open.

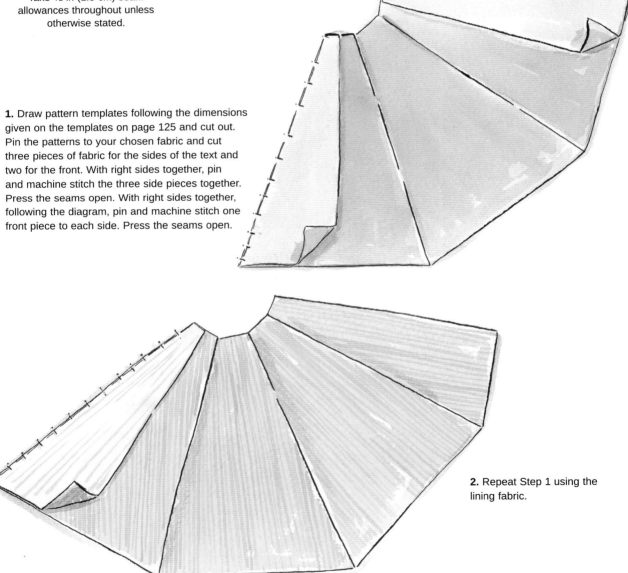

2. Repeat Step 1 using the lining fabric.

3. With right sides together, pin and machine stitch the two front panels together from the top down for a distance of about 36 in (90 cm). Press the seam open. Repeat on the lining fabric.

4. With right sides together, pin the lining to the main fabric around the bottom edge, matching the seams of both fabrics. Machine stitch in place, leaving a gap of 1 in (2.5 cm) at either side of each seam and stitching around the opening for the door. Snip the seam at the top of the door opening and turn the tent right side out.

5. On the main fabric, press under ½ in (1.5 cm) around the top of the tent and machine stitch in place. Repeat with the lining fabric. Pin, baste (tack), and machine stitch a line from the bottom to the top of the tent 1 in (2.5 cm) from each seam to form four corner channels.

6. Hand stitch around the top of the tent between the channels to join the main fabric and lining fabrics together.

7. Cut a 20 in (50 cm) length of ribbon. Measure halfway along it and machine stitch it onto the tent 2 in (5 cm) from the top, in the center of the back panel of the tent.

8. Cut four 12 in (30 cm) lengths of ribbon. Machine stitch one ribbon to the bottom corner of each door opening, folding under ½ in (1.5 cm) at the end. Stitch the remaining two ribbons onto the seam between the front and side panels 21½ in (55 cm) from the bottom of the tent, taking care not to stitch through the channel.

9. Push the dowelling poles up through the corner channels and push the bottom ends of the poles into the ground slightly so that the side panels are pulled flat. (You may need an extra pair of hands for this!) Gather up the top of the tent around the poles and tie the ribbon several times around it, tying with a bow to secure.

Pet basket

3 hours

This cute animal basket makes the perfect bed for your pet. The size given here is suitable for a cat or small dog, but it can easily be increased in size for larger dogs. The toy, which is made from scraps of fabric, will keep your pet company while the cord that fastens it to the basket will ensure that it never strays too far away. You could even fill the toy with catnip to make the perfect playmate for your feline friend.

YOU WILL NEED

40 in (1 m) patterned fabric

Paper for pattern

Pencil and string

Drawing pin

Templates on page 126

Sewing machine and matching sewing thread

Scraps of fabric for the toy

Stuffing

2 small buttons

8 in (20 cm) length of ribbon for bow

Thick washable batting (wadding)

Take ½ in (1.5 cm) seam allowances throughout unless otherwise stated.

1. Fold a piece of paper in half and then into quarters. Tie a piece of string around a pencil. Pin the string to the folded corner of the paper, leaving a 9½ in (24 cm) length of string. Draw a quarter circle on the paper and cut out. This will be the paper pattern for the base of the basket. Lay the paper pattern on a double thickness of patterned fabric and cut out.

2. Use the side-panel template on page 126 to make a paper pattern (see page 119). Pin the paper pattern onto your chosen fabric and cut out. With right sides together, pin and machine stitch the ends together and press open the seam.

3. With right sides together, pin and stitch the side panel onto one of the base circles. Make small snips all the way around the seam allowance and press the seam open.

4. To make the toy, cut a 3½ x 5 in (9 x 13 cm) piece of plain fabric, a 2 x 5 in (5 x 13 cm). strip of patterned fabric and a 2¼ x 5 in (6 x 13 cm) strip of patterned fabric. With right sides together, pin and machine stitch the strips together. Trace the toy template on page 126 onto paper and cut out. Pin the pattern onto the fabric panel and cut out. Then pin the paper pattern onto plain fabric and cut out. Cut four arms from patterned fabric.

5. With right sides together, stitch two arm pieces together, leaving the straight side open. Fill with stuffing. Repeat with the remaining two arm pieces. Pin the two pieces for the toy together with the arms in between, aligning the raw edges. Stitch all around, leaving a 1½ in (4 cm) gap in one side. Turn right side out and fill with stuffing. Stitch the opening closed and sew on buttons for eyes and a bow at the neck.

6. Cut a 31 x 2½ in (78 x 6 cm) strip of patterned fabric. Fold it in half lengthwise, wrong sides together, and then fold the raw edges in to the center crease. Machine stitch along the length, stitching as close to the edge as possible.

7. Using the template, cut out the inner side panel. With right sides together, pin and machine stitch the ends together and press open the seam. Pin and machine stitch the inner side panel onto the remaining base circle, inserting one end of the fabric ribbon into the seam, and leaving an opening of about 8 in (20 cm) Make small snips all the way around the seam allowance. Press.

8. With right sides together, pin and machine stitch the outer side panel to the inner panel. Make small snips around the curved sections and turn right side out. Press.

9. Using the paper patterns that you cut earlier, cut out batting (wadding) pieces and insert them through the opening into the base and around the sides to form a basket shape. Hand stitch the opening closed and sew the toy onto the end of the fabric ribbon. Make a few stitches around the inside base of the basket through all the layers to hold the batting in place.

Techniques and templates

Techniques

The sewing techniques used in this book are all very simple, allowing you to create stylish soft furnishings and accessories for your home quickly and easily. You need only minimal equipment—sharp scissors for cutting fabric and thread, a selection of hand-sewing needles, tailor's chalk, some tracing paper, a pencil or fabric marker pen, and a basic sewing machine.

ENLARGING MOTIFS

Although books and patterns often give motifs at actual size, it is useful to know how to enlarge them.

First, decide how big you want the motif to be on the finished garment. Let's say, for example, that you want a particular shape to be 20 in (50 cm) tall.

Then measure the template that you are working from. Let's imagine that the template is smaller than the size you require—say, 10 in (25 cm) tall.

Take the size that you want the motif to be (20 in/50 cm) and divide it by the actual size of the template (10 in/25 cm). Multiply that figure by 100 and you get 200—so you need to enlarge the motif on a photocopier to 200%.

REDUCING MOTIFS

If you want a motif on the finished piece to be smaller than the template, the process is exactly the same.

For example, if the template is 10 in (25 cm) tall and you want the motif to be 8 in (20 cm) tall, divide 8 in (20 cm) by the actual size of the template (10 in/25 cm) and multiply by 100, which gives you a figure of 80. So the figure that you need to key in on the photocopier is 80%.

USING TEMPLATES AND PATTERNS

Several of the projects in this book require you to make a template or pattern that you can draw around to cut out a corresponding fabric shape.

1. Using a thick black pencil, trace the motif onto tracing paper.

2. Turn the tracing paper over, place it on card, and scribble over your drawn lines to transfer them to the card.

3. Finally, cut out the card shape using scissors or a craft knife on a cutting mat. You can now place the card template on your chosen fabric and draw around it with tailor's chalk or a fabric marker pencil to transfer the shape to the fabric.

HAND STITCHES

These are the most common hand stitches used for joining (either temporarily or permanently) two pieces of fabric together.

BASTING (TACKING) STITCH

This stitch is used to temporarily hold pieces of fabric in place until they have been sewn together permanently. Basting stitches are removed once the permanent stitching is complete. It's a good idea to use a contrasting color of thread, so that you can see it easily.

Knot the thread and work a long running stitch through all layers of fabric.

Basting (tacking) stitch

RUNNING STITCH

Running stitch is probably the simplest hand stitch of all. It is often used to gather a strip of fabric into a frill.

Work from right to left.

Bring the needle up at (a) on the front of the fabric. Take it down again at (b) and up again at (c). Repeat as required.

SLIPSTITCH

This stitch is almost invisible and is an easy method of hemming. It is also used to close openings—for example, when you've left one side of a pillow cover open for turning right side out.

Work from right to left.

Slide the needle between the two pieces of fabric, bringing it out on the edge of the top fabric so that the knot in the thread is hidden between the two layers. Pick up one or two threads from the base fabric, then bring the needle up a short distance along, on the edge of the top fabric, and pull through. Repeat as required.

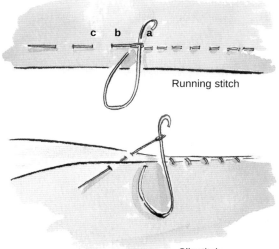

Running stitch

Slipstitch

FASTENINGS

Buttons and zippers are the most common fastenings. Modern sewing machines take the hard work out of making buttonholes and inserting zippers.

MACHINE-STITCHED BUTTONHOLES

Different sewing machines tend to use slightly different methods for stitching buttonholes, so follow the manufacturer's instructions for your particular machine.

1. Mark the size of the required buttonhole on the fabric with tailor's chalk or similar. Machine stitch a tight line of zigzag stitches along each side of the marked line, with a block of stitches at either end. Most sewing machines have a special buttonhole foot, which enables you to do this.

2. Using small, sharp scissors or a seam ripper, cut a slit between the lines of zigzag stitches.

INSERTING A ZIPPER

With this method, the zipper is almost invisible. Choose a zipper tape in a color that matches your fabric.

1. With right sides together, pin the two fabric pieces together along the seam allowance. Measure the length of the zipper and mark a space centrally on the fabric to this measurement. Stitch from each end of the fabric to the mark for the opening. Baste (tack) the open section of the fabric and press the seam open.

2. Lay the closed zipper right side down along the basted (tacked) area on the wrong side of the fabric and baste in place. Using the zipper foot on your machine, topstitch the zipper in place on the right side of the fabric evenly down both sides and across both ends. Remove the basting stitches and open the zipper.

TOPSTITCHING

Topstitching is a name for a longer straight stitch (around 3–4 on your sewing machine's stitch length indicator). It is often used to finish an edge—as well as being decorative, it prevents the underside of the edge from rolling to the outside. Working from the right side, line up your finished seam edge on the chosen guideline and begin stitching, turning any corners by lifting your presser foot and pivoting your fabric around the needle. Trim your thread ends even with the raw edges.

Templates

Add a ½ in (1.5 cm) seam allowance all around each piece when cutting out.

Drawstring toy bags

Page 60
(actual size)

Peg bag

Page 94
Enlarge by 195%

Cutting line for bottom section of front

Cutting line for top section of front

Padded coat hanger

Page 98

Coat hanger

Enlarge by 236%

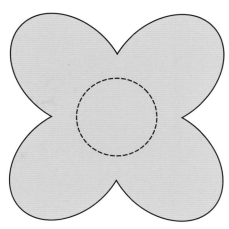

Small flower

(actual size)

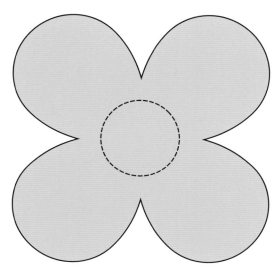

Large flower

(actual size)

Awning

Page 102
Enlarge by 115%

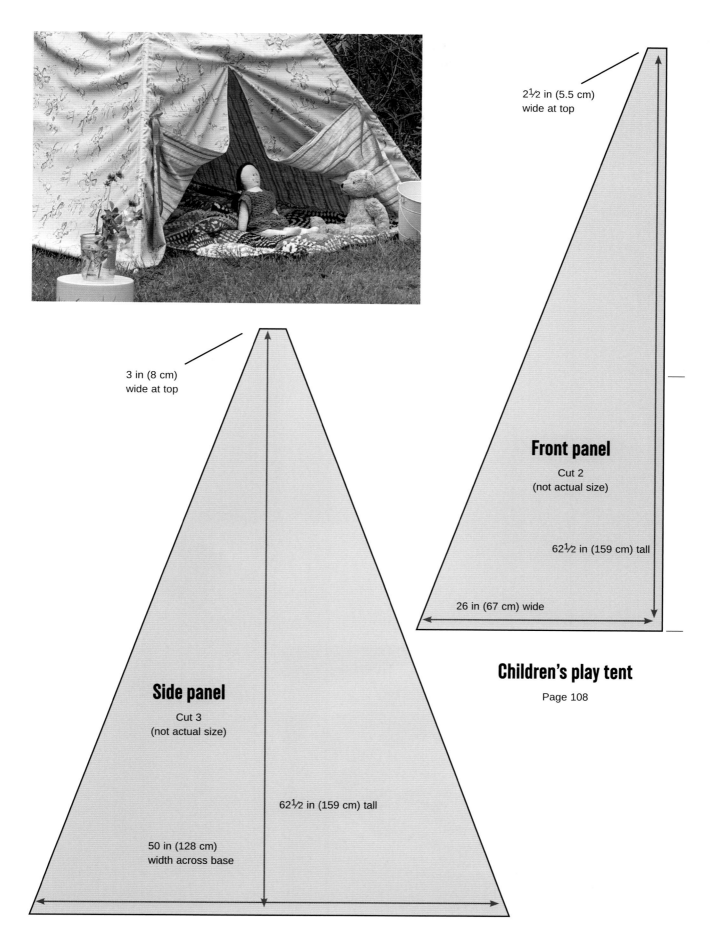

2½ in (5.5 cm) wide at top

3 in (8 cm) wide at top

Front panel

Cut 2
(not actual size)

62½ in (159 cm) tall

26 in (67 cm) wide

Children's play tent

Page 108

Side panel

Cut 3
(not actual size)

62½ in (159 cm) tall

50 in (128 cm) width across base

Pet basket toy

Page 112
(actual size)

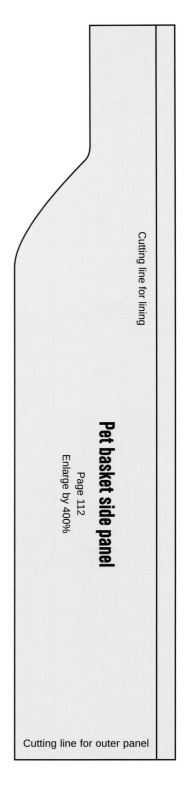

Cutting line for lining

Pet basket side panel

Page 112
Enlarge by 400%

Cutting line for outer panel

Suppliers

US SUPPLIERS

Amy Butler
For stockists, see
www.amybutlerdesign.com

Britex Fabrics
117 Post Street
San Francisco
CA 94108
415 392 2910
www.britexfabrics.com

Good Yard Goods
4155 Grand Ave S.
Minneapolis
MN 55409
612 806 6191
www.goodyardgoods.com

Purl Soho
800 597 PURL
www.purlsoho.com

Tinsel Trading
1659 San Pablo Avenue
Berkeley
CA 94702
510 570 2149
www.tinseltrading.com

UK SUPPLIERS

The Button Queen
0207 935 1505
www.thebuttonqueen.co.uk

Laura Ashley
0333 777 8000
www.next.co.uk/laura-ashley

John Lewis
300 Oxford Street
London
W1C 1DX
020 7629 7711
www.johnlewis.com

Liberty
Regent Street
London
W1B 5AH
020 3893 3062
www.liberty.co.uk

Ian Mankin
Studio Two, Worlds End Studios
Lots Road
London
SW10 0RJ
020 7722 0997
www.ianmankin.com

Cloth House
130 Royal College Street
London
NW1 0TA
020 7485 6247
www.clothhouse.com

Cath Kidston
0333 777 8000
www.next.co.uk/cath-kidston

VV Rouleaux
102 Marylebone Lane
London
W1U 2QD
0207 224 5179
www.vvrouleaux.com

Acknowledgments

I would like to thank everyone who worked on this book, especially Debbie Patterson for the beautiful photography and for making the shoots a lot of fun, Sarah Hoggett for editing the book with such calm and patience, Michael Hill for the lovely illustrations, and David Fordham for the great design. At CICO, I would like to thank Sally Powell for all her assistance and support, and Cindy Richards for giving me the opportunity to do the book. You have all helped to make it a really enjoyable project.

Thank you to Maria Dahl for the loan of some lovely props. And thank you, thank you, thank you to Laurie for sharing our home with piles and piles of fabric, ribbons, and buttons and still being enthusiastic about the whole project. A huge thank you to Gracie and Betty, my gorgeous girls, for giving me so many great ideas and lots of inspiration and for getting as excited about fabrics, notions, and making things as I do. You are stars!

Index